WALL ART MADE

Vincent van Gogh

30 Ready to Frame Reproduction Prints

Barbara Ann Kirby

ISBN-9781709349386

INTRODUCTION

Wall Art Made Easy: Vincent van Gogh: 30 Ready to Frame Reproduction Prints features thirty prints of paintings by Vincent Willem van Gogh (1853-1890), the most famous Dutch post-impressionist painter of all time.

Within these pages, you will find thirty vibrant full color portrait and landscape oriented prints of some of his most famous paintings including The Starry Night, Sunflowers, Irises, Bedroom in Arles, Wheat Field with Cypresses as well as many more beautiful artworks.

If you're a fan of Vincent van Gogh you're sure to find some that you'll love enough to want to display on your walls in all their glory.

Each image is ideal for a 8" x 10" frame with a 1" mat and can be easily removed from the book by cutting along the line shown on the page.

Easily transform your home décor using *Wall Art Made Easy: Vincent van Gogh: 30 Ready to Frame Reproduction Prints*, the far cheaper alternative to buying expensive prints!

First Steps

Cypresses

Irises

Sunflowers

Irises

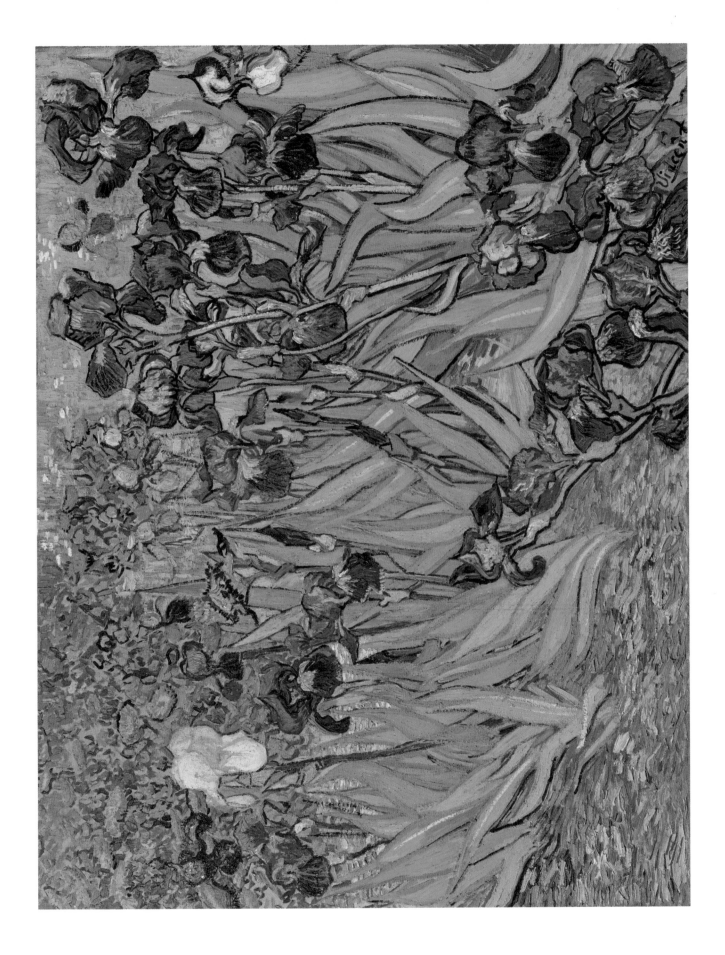

Wheat Field with Cypresses

Olive Trees

Shoes

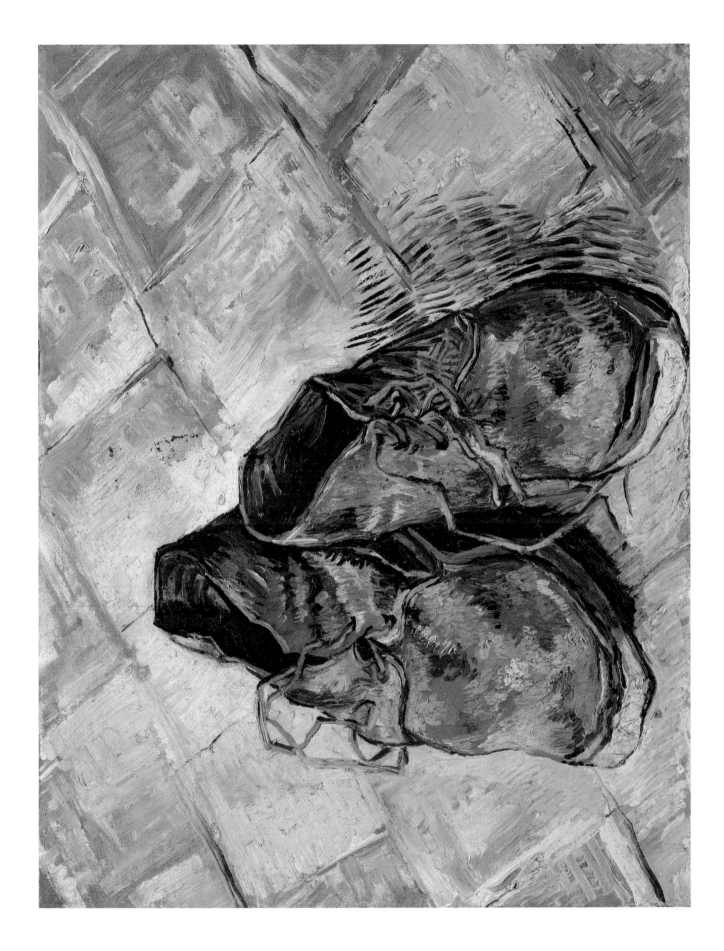

The Flowering Orchard

Bouquet of Flowers in a Vase

Fishing in Spring

Grapes, Lemons, Pears and Apples

La Berceuse

Houses and Figure

The Factory

Le Café de Nuit

The Poplars at Saint-Rémy

Green Wheat Fields, Auvers

Self portrait

Farmhouse in Provence

Still Life

Square Saint-Pierre, Paris

The Starry Night

Terrace and Observation Deck at the Moulin de Blute-Fin, Montmartre

Bedroom in Arles

The Drinkers

The Poet's Garden

Roses

Self portrait

Orchard Bordered by Cypresses

Other Titles in the **"Masters of Art Series"**:

Renoir

Rembrandt

Raphael

Rubens

Paul Gauguin

Diego Velázquez

Pieter Bruegel the Elder

Wallartmadeeasy.com